50 Raw Food Recipes for Home

By: Kelly Johnson

Table of Contents

- Zucchini Noodles with Avocado Sauce
- Raw Vegan Tacos
- Spicy Cauliflower Buffalo Wings
- Raw Vegetable Spring Rolls
- Beet and Carrot Salad with Lemon Dressing
- Raw Chocolate Avocado Pudding
- Spinach and Mango Salad
- Cashew Cream Cheese Spread
- Raw Vegan Sushi
- Marinated Mushroom Salad
- Chia Seed Pudding with Berries
- Raw Carrot and Ginger Soup
- Sweet Potato and Avocado Salad
- Raw Coconut Macaroons
- Stuffed Bell Peppers with Quinoa
- Raw Energy Balls
- Garden Gazpacho
- Raw Cacao Bliss Balls
- Mango Coconut Chia Pudding
- Raw Chocolate-Covered Almonds
- Raw Kale Salad with Lemon-Tahini Dressing
- Coconut-Lime Raw Bars
- Raw Veggie Platter with Hummus
- Raw Lemon Bars
- Spicy Almonds and Walnuts
- Raw Chocolate Chip Cookies
- Fresh Fruit Tart with Nut Crust
- Raw Falafel with Tahini Sauce
- Raw Granola with Nut Milk
- Rainbow Salad with Citrus Dressing
- Raw Vegan Cheese Platter
- Creamy Avocado Dressing
- Raw Peach Crisp
- Raw Cabbage Slaw with Sesame Dressing
- Raw Nut Burgers

- Coconut Water and Berry Smoothie
- Raw Zucchini Fritters
- Raw Berry Pie
- Marinated Avocado Salad
- Raw Chocolate Energy Bars
- Raw Pumpkin Seed Hummus
- Fresh Herb Pesto
- Raw Choco-Nut Brownies
- Spicy Watermelon Salad
- Raw Nutty Granola Bars
- Tropical Fruit Salad
- Raw Chocolate Banana Ice Cream
- Raw Sweet Potato Chips
- Raw Almond Milk
- Raw Pumpkin Pie Smoothie

Zucchini Noodles with Avocado Sauce

Ingredients

- 2 medium zucchinis, spiralized
- 1 ripe avocado
- 2 tablespoons lemon juice
- 2 tablespoons olive oil
- 1 garlic clove
- Salt and pepper, to taste
- Cherry tomatoes, halved (for garnish)

Instructions

1. **Make the Sauce:**
   - In a blender, combine avocado, lemon juice, olive oil, garlic, salt, and pepper. Blend until smooth.
2. **Prepare Zoodles:**
   - Toss the spiralized zucchini with the avocado sauce until well coated.
3. **Serve:**
   - Garnish with cherry tomatoes and enjoy!

Raw Vegan Tacos

Ingredients

- 1 cup walnuts, soaked
- 1 tablespoon taco seasoning
- 1 cup diced tomatoes
- 1/2 cup corn (fresh or frozen)
- 1 avocado, diced
- Lettuce leaves (for shells)

Instructions

1. **Prepare Walnut Filling:**
   - In a food processor, blend soaked walnuts and taco seasoning until crumbly.
2. **Assemble Tacos:**
   - Fill lettuce leaves with walnut mixture, diced tomatoes, corn, and avocado.
3. **Serve:**
   - Enjoy your fresh and crunchy tacos!

Spicy Cauliflower Buffalo Wings

Ingredients

- 1 head cauliflower, cut into florets
- 1 cup almond flour
- 1/2 cup water
- 1 tablespoon garlic powder
- 1 tablespoon onion powder
- 1/2 cup hot sauce
- 1 tablespoon olive oil

Instructions

1. **Preheat Oven:**
    - Preheat your oven to 450°F (230°C) and line a baking sheet with parchment paper.
2. **Prepare Batter:**
    - In a bowl, mix almond flour, water, garlic powder, and onion powder to form a batter.
3. **Coat Cauliflower:**
    - Dip each cauliflower floret into the batter and place on the baking sheet.
4. **Bake:**
    - Bake for 20-25 minutes until golden and crispy.
5. **Coat in Hot Sauce:**
    - In a bowl, mix baked cauliflower with hot sauce and olive oil. Bake for an additional 10 minutes.
6. **Serve:**
    - Enjoy with your favorite dipping sauce!

Raw Vegetable Spring Rolls

Ingredients

- Rice paper wraps
- 1 cup mixed vegetables (carrots, cucumber, bell pepper, etc.), julienned
- Fresh herbs (mint, cilantro, basil)
- Dipping sauce (soy sauce, peanut sauce, or sweet chili sauce)

Instructions

1. **Soak Rice Paper:**
    - Soak rice paper wraps in warm water for a few seconds until pliable.
2. **Fill Wraps:**
    - Layer vegetables and herbs on the wrap, then roll tightly.
3. **Serve:**
    - Serve with your choice of dipping sauce.

Beet and Carrot Salad with Lemon Dressing

Ingredients

- 2 medium beets, cooked and diced
- 2 large carrots, grated
- 2 tablespoons olive oil
- Juice of 1 lemon
- Salt and pepper, to taste
- Fresh parsley, chopped (for garnish)

Instructions

1. **Mix Dressing:**
   - In a bowl, whisk together olive oil, lemon juice, salt, and pepper.
2. **Combine Salad:**
   - In a large bowl, mix diced beets, grated carrots, and dressing until well combined.
3. **Serve:**
   - Garnish with fresh parsley and enjoy!

Raw Chocolate Avocado Pudding

Ingredients

- 2 ripe avocados
- 1/4 cup cocoa powder
- 1/4 cup maple syrup
- 1 teaspoon vanilla extract
- Pinch of salt

Instructions

1. **Blend Ingredients:**
   - In a food processor, combine avocados, cocoa powder, maple syrup, vanilla, and salt. Blend until smooth.
2. **Chill:**
   - Refrigerate for at least 30 minutes.
3. **Serve:**
   - Enjoy as a rich and creamy dessert!

Spinach and Mango Salad

Ingredients

- 4 cups fresh spinach
- 1 ripe mango, diced
- 1/4 red onion, thinly sliced
- 1/4 cup walnuts or pecans
- Dressing: 2 tablespoons olive oil, 1 tablespoon apple cider vinegar, salt, and pepper

Instructions

1. **Combine Salad Ingredients:**
    - In a large bowl, mix spinach, mango, red onion, and nuts.
2. **Prepare Dressing:**
    - In a small bowl, whisk together olive oil, apple cider vinegar, salt, and pepper.
3. **Dress Salad:**
    - Drizzle dressing over the salad and toss gently.
4. **Serve:**
    - Enjoy your refreshing salad!

Cashew Cream Cheese Spread

Ingredients

- 1 cup raw cashews, soaked for 2-4 hours
- 2 tablespoons lemon juice
- 1 teaspoon garlic powder
- Salt, to taste
- Fresh herbs (chives or dill, optional)

Instructions

1. **Blend Cashews:**
    - Drain and rinse soaked cashews. In a blender, combine with lemon juice, garlic powder, and salt. Blend until smooth.
2. **Add Herbs (if using):**
    - Fold in fresh herbs for added flavor.
3. **Chill:**
    - Refrigerate for at least 30 minutes before serving.
4. **Serve:**
    - Enjoy as a spread on crackers or vegetables!

Enjoy these vibrant and healthy recipes!

Raw Vegan Sushi

Ingredients

- Nori sheets
- 1 cup cauliflower, grated
- 1 carrot, julienned
- 1 cucumber, julienned
- 1 avocado, sliced
- 1/2 bell pepper, julienned
- Soy sauce or tamari (for dipping)

Instructions

1. **Prepare Cauliflower Rice:**
   - Grate cauliflower to make "rice."
2. **Assemble Sushi:**
   - On a nori sheet, spread a thin layer of cauliflower rice. Layer with carrot, cucumber, avocado, and bell pepper.
3. **Roll:**
   - Roll the nori tightly, then slice into bite-sized pieces.
4. **Serve:**
   - Enjoy with soy sauce or tamari for dipping!

Marinated Mushroom Salad

Ingredients

- 2 cups mixed mushrooms (button, shiitake, etc.), sliced
- 3 tablespoons olive oil
- 2 tablespoons balsamic vinegar
- 1 garlic clove, minced
- Salt and pepper, to taste
- Fresh parsley, chopped (for garnish)

Instructions

1. **Marinate Mushrooms:**
    - In a bowl, combine olive oil, balsamic vinegar, garlic, salt, and pepper. Add mushrooms and toss to coat.
2. **Let Sit:**
    - Allow mushrooms to marinate for at least 30 minutes.
3. **Serve:**
    - Garnish with fresh parsley and enjoy!

Chia Seed Pudding with Berries

Ingredients

- 1/4 cup chia seeds
- 1 cup almond milk (or any plant milk)
- 2 tablespoons maple syrup (optional)
- 1/2 teaspoon vanilla extract
- Fresh berries (for topping)

Instructions

1. **Combine Ingredients:**
    - In a bowl, whisk together chia seeds, almond milk, maple syrup, and vanilla.
2. **Refrigerate:**
    - Let sit in the fridge for at least 4 hours or overnight until thickened.
3. **Serve:**
    - Top with fresh berries before serving.

Raw Carrot and Ginger Soup

Ingredients

- 2 cups carrots, chopped
- 1 inch fresh ginger, peeled and chopped
- 1 cup vegetable broth
- 1 tablespoon lemon juice
- Salt and pepper, to taste

Instructions

1. **Blend Ingredients:**
   - In a blender, combine carrots, ginger, vegetable broth, lemon juice, salt, and pepper. Blend until smooth.
2. **Chill:**
   - Refrigerate for at least 1 hour before serving.
3. **Serve:**
   - Enjoy chilled or at room temperature.

Sweet Potato and Avocado Salad

Ingredients

- 1 large sweet potato, roasted and diced
- 1 avocado, diced
- 2 cups mixed greens
- 1/4 red onion, thinly sliced
- Dressing: 2 tablespoons olive oil, 1 tablespoon apple cider vinegar, salt, and pepper

Instructions

1. **Combine Salad Ingredients:**
    - In a bowl, mix roasted sweet potato, avocado, mixed greens, and red onion.
2. **Prepare Dressing:**
    - In a small bowl, whisk together olive oil, apple cider vinegar, salt, and pepper.
3. **Dress Salad:**
    - Drizzle dressing over the salad and toss gently.
4. **Serve:**
    - Enjoy your vibrant salad!

Raw Coconut Macaroons

Ingredients

- 2 cups shredded coconut
- 1/2 cup almond flour
- 1/4 cup maple syrup
- 1 teaspoon vanilla extract

Instructions

1. **Mix Ingredients:**
    - In a bowl, combine shredded coconut, almond flour, maple syrup, and vanilla. Mix until well combined.
2. **Form Macaroons:**
    - Scoop out portions and roll into balls.
3. **Chill:**
    - Refrigerate for at least 30 minutes to set.
4. **Serve:**
    - Enjoy these sweet treats!

Stuffed Bell Peppers with Quinoa

Ingredients

- 4 bell peppers, halved and seeded
- 1 cup cooked quinoa
- 1 cup black beans, rinsed and drained
- 1 cup corn (fresh or frozen)
- 1 teaspoon cumin
- Salt and pepper, to taste
- Fresh cilantro (for garnish)

Instructions

1. **Preheat Oven:**
    - Preheat your oven to 375°F (190°C).
2. **Prepare Filling:**
    - In a bowl, mix cooked quinoa, black beans, corn, cumin, salt, and pepper.
3. **Stuff Peppers:**
    - Fill each bell pepper half with the quinoa mixture.
4. **Bake:**
    - Place stuffed peppers in a baking dish and bake for 25-30 minutes.
5. **Serve:**
    - Garnish with fresh cilantro and enjoy!

Raw Energy Balls

Ingredients

- 1 cup pitted dates
- 1 cup nuts (almonds, walnuts, etc.)
- 1/4 cup cacao nibs or chocolate chips
- 1 tablespoon chia seeds
- 1 teaspoon vanilla extract

Instructions

1. **Blend Ingredients:**
    - In a food processor, blend dates, nuts, cacao nibs, chia seeds, and vanilla until a sticky mixture forms.
2. **Form Balls:**
    - Scoop out portions and roll into balls.
3. **Chill:**
    - Refrigerate for at least 30 minutes to set.
4. **Serve:**
    - Enjoy these energizing snacks!

Enjoy these fresh and nutritious recipes!

Garden Gazpacho

Ingredients

- 4 ripe tomatoes, chopped
- 1 cucumber, peeled and chopped
- 1 bell pepper, chopped
- 1/2 red onion, chopped
- 2 cloves garlic, minced
- 2 cups tomato juice
- 2 tablespoons olive oil
- 2 tablespoons red wine vinegar
- Salt and pepper, to taste
- Fresh basil (for garnish)

Instructions

1. **Blend Ingredients:**
   - In a blender, combine tomatoes, cucumber, bell pepper, red onion, garlic, tomato juice, olive oil, red wine vinegar, salt, and pepper. Blend until smooth.
2. **Chill:**
   - Refrigerate for at least 1 hour to allow flavors to meld.
3. **Serve:**
   - Garnish with fresh basil before serving.

Raw Cacao Bliss Balls

Ingredients

- 1 cup pitted dates
- 1/2 cup nuts (almonds or walnuts)
- 1/4 cup raw cacao powder
- 1 tablespoon coconut oil
- 1 teaspoon vanilla extract
- Pinch of salt

Instructions

1. **Blend Ingredients:**
   - In a food processor, combine dates, nuts, cacao powder, coconut oil, vanilla, and salt. Blend until a sticky mixture forms.
2. **Form Balls:**
   - Scoop out portions and roll into balls.
3. **Chill:**
   - Refrigerate for at least 30 minutes to set.
4. **Serve:**
   - Enjoy these chocolatey treats!

Mango Coconut Chia Pudding

Ingredients

- 1/4 cup chia seeds
- 1 cup coconut milk
- 1 tablespoon maple syrup (optional)
- 1 ripe mango, diced

Instructions

1. **Combine Ingredients:**
   - In a bowl, whisk together chia seeds, coconut milk, and maple syrup.
2. **Refrigerate:**
   - Let sit in the fridge for at least 4 hours or overnight until thickened.
3. **Serve:**
   - Top with diced mango before serving.

Raw Chocolate-Covered Almonds

Ingredients

- 1 cup raw almonds
- 1 cup dark chocolate chips
- 1 tablespoon coconut oil
- Sea salt (for sprinkling, optional)

Instructions

1. **Melt Chocolate:**
    - In a microwave-safe bowl, melt chocolate chips and coconut oil in 30-second intervals until smooth.
2. **Coat Almonds:**
    - Dip each almond into the melted chocolate and place on a lined baking sheet.
3. **Sprinkle with Salt:**
    - If desired, sprinkle with sea salt.
4. **Chill:**
    - Refrigerate until the chocolate hardens, then enjoy!

Raw Kale Salad with Lemon-Tahini Dressing

Ingredients

- 4 cups kale, chopped
- 1/4 cup tahini
- 2 tablespoons lemon juice
- 1 tablespoon olive oil
- 1 tablespoon maple syrup
- Salt and pepper, to taste
- 1/4 cup sunflower seeds (for topping)

Instructions

1. **Make Dressing:**
    - In a bowl, whisk together tahini, lemon juice, olive oil, maple syrup, salt, and pepper.
2. **Massage Kale:**
    - Pour dressing over kale and massage for a few minutes until wilted.
3. **Serve:**
    - Top with sunflower seeds and enjoy!

Coconut-Lime Raw Bars

Ingredients

- 1 cup almond flour
- 1 cup shredded coconut
- 1/4 cup maple syrup
- Zest of 1 lime
- Juice of 1 lime

Instructions

1. **Mix Ingredients:**
   - In a bowl, combine almond flour, shredded coconut, maple syrup, lime zest, and lime juice. Mix until well combined.
2. **Press into Pan:**
   - Press the mixture into a lined baking dish.
3. **Chill:**
   - Refrigerate for at least 1 hour to set.
4. **Cut and Serve:**
   - Cut into bars and enjoy!

Raw Veggie Platter with Hummus

Ingredients

- Assorted raw vegetables (carrots, cucumbers, bell peppers, celery)
- 1 cup hummus (store-bought or homemade)

Instructions

1. **Prepare Vegetables:**
     - Slice vegetables into sticks or bite-sized pieces.
2. **Serve:**
     - Arrange on a platter with hummus for dipping. Enjoy your healthy snack!

Raw Lemon Bars

Ingredients

- 1 cup pitted dates
- 1 cup almond flour
- 1/4 cup lemon juice
- Zest of 1 lemon
- 1/4 cup coconut oil, melted

Instructions

1. **Blend Base:**
   - In a food processor, blend dates and almond flour until crumbly. Press into a lined baking dish.
2. **Mix Filling:**
   - In a bowl, combine lemon juice, lemon zest, and melted coconut oil. Pour over the base.
3. **Chill:**
   - Refrigerate for at least 2 hours to set.
4. **Cut and Serve:**
   - Cut into squares and enjoy!

Enjoy these fresh and vibrant recipes!

Spicy Almonds and Walnuts

Ingredients

- 1 cup raw almonds
- 1 cup raw walnuts
- 2 tablespoons olive oil
- 1 teaspoon smoked paprika
- 1/2 teaspoon cayenne pepper (adjust to taste)
- 1 teaspoon garlic powder
- Salt, to taste

Instructions

1. **Preheat Oven:**
    - Preheat your oven to 350°F (175°C).
2. **Toss Nuts:**
    - In a bowl, mix almonds and walnuts with olive oil, smoked paprika, cayenne, garlic powder, and salt.
3. **Roast:**
    - Spread the mixture on a baking sheet and roast for 10-12 minutes, stirring halfway through.
4. **Cool:**
    - Let cool before serving.

Raw Chocolate Chip Cookies

Ingredients

- 1 cup almond flour
- 1/2 cup pitted dates
- 1/4 cup coconut oil, melted
- 1/4 cup raw cacao nibs
- 1 teaspoon vanilla extract
- Pinch of salt

Instructions

1. **Blend Ingredients:**
   - In a food processor, combine almond flour, dates, melted coconut oil, vanilla, and salt. Blend until a dough forms.
2. **Fold in Cacao Nibs:**
   - Stir in cacao nibs.
3. **Form Cookies:**
   - Scoop out portions and shape into cookies. Place on a lined baking sheet.
4. **Chill:**
   - Refrigerate for at least 30 minutes before serving.

Fresh Fruit Tart with Nut Crust

Ingredients

- 1 cup mixed nuts (almonds, walnuts, pecans)
- 1/2 cup pitted dates
- 2 tablespoons coconut oil, melted
- 2 cups mixed fresh fruit (berries, kiwi, mango, etc.)
- 1/4 cup coconut yogurt (for filling)

Instructions

1. **Prepare Crust:**
    - In a food processor, blend nuts and dates until crumbly. Add melted coconut oil and blend until combined.
2. **Press into Pan:**
    - Press the mixture into the bottom of a tart pan to form the crust.
3. **Assemble Tart:**
    - Spread coconut yogurt over the crust and top with fresh fruit.
4. **Serve:**
    - Chill before serving.

Raw Falafel with Tahini Sauce

Ingredients

- 1 cup chickpeas, soaked
- 1/2 cup parsley, chopped
- 1/4 cup onion, chopped
- 2 cloves garlic
- 1 teaspoon cumin
- Salt and pepper, to taste

Tahini Sauce

- 1/4 cup tahini
- 2 tablespoons lemon juice
- Water (to thin)
- Salt, to taste

Instructions

1. **Blend Falafel Ingredients:**
   - In a food processor, combine soaked chickpeas, parsley, onion, garlic, cumin, salt, and pepper. Blend until a coarse mixture forms.
2. **Form Balls:**
   - Shape into small balls and place on a plate.
3. **Make Tahini Sauce:**
   - In a bowl, mix tahini, lemon juice, water, and salt until smooth.
4. **Serve:**
   - Serve falafel with tahini sauce for dipping.

Raw Granola with Nut Milk

Ingredients

- 1 cup rolled oats
- 1/2 cup nuts (almonds, walnuts, etc.), chopped
- 1/4 cup seeds (pumpkin, sunflower)
- 1/4 cup dried fruit (raisins, cranberries)
- 1/4 cup maple syrup
- 1 teaspoon vanilla extract

Instructions

1. **Combine Ingredients:**
   - In a bowl, mix oats, nuts, seeds, dried fruit, maple syrup, and vanilla until well combined.
2. **Dehydrate (optional):**
   - For a crunchy texture, dehydrate in a dehydrator or low oven for a few hours.
3. **Serve:**
   - Enjoy with nut milk!

Rainbow Salad with Citrus Dressing

Ingredients

- 4 cups mixed greens
- 1 cup cherry tomatoes, halved
- 1 cup bell peppers, chopped
- 1 cup cucumber, sliced
- 1 cup shredded carrots
- 1 avocado, sliced

Dressing

- 1/4 cup olive oil
- Juice of 1 orange
- Juice of 1 lemon
- Salt and pepper, to taste

Instructions

1. **Prepare Dressing:**
    - In a bowl, whisk together olive oil, orange juice, lemon juice, salt, and pepper.
2. **Combine Salad Ingredients:**
    - In a large bowl, mix greens, tomatoes, bell peppers, cucumber, carrots, and avocado.
3. **Dress Salad:**
    - Drizzle with dressing and toss gently.
4. **Serve:**
    - Enjoy your colorful salad!

Raw Vegan Cheese Platter

Ingredients

- 1 cup cashews, soaked
- 2 tablespoons nutritional yeast
- 1 tablespoon lemon juice
- 1 clove garlic
- Salt, to taste
- Assorted crackers and fresh fruits for serving

Instructions

1. **Blend Cheese Ingredients:**
    - In a food processor, combine soaked cashews, nutritional yeast, lemon juice, garlic, and salt. Blend until smooth.
2. **Chill:**
    - Refrigerate for at least 30 minutes to firm up.
3. **Serve:**
    - Serve with crackers and fresh fruits.

Creamy Avocado Dressing

Ingredients

- 1 ripe avocado
- 1/4 cup olive oil
- 2 tablespoons lemon juice
- 1 clove garlic
- Salt and pepper, to taste
- Water (to thin, as needed)

Instructions

1. **Blend Ingredients:**
   - In a blender, combine avocado, olive oil, lemon juice, garlic, salt, and pepper. Blend until smooth.
2. **Adjust Consistency:**
   - Add water to reach desired consistency.
3. **Serve:**
   - Drizzle over salads or use as a dip!

Enjoy these delicious and healthy recipes!

Raw Peach Crisp

Ingredients

- 2 cups fresh peaches, sliced
- 1 cup almond flour
- 1/2 cup pitted dates
- 1/2 cup rolled oats
- 1/4 cup shredded coconut
- 1 teaspoon cinnamon

Instructions

1. **Prepare Filling:**
    - In a bowl, combine sliced peaches with a sprinkle of cinnamon. Set aside.
2. **Make Crisp Topping:**
    - In a food processor, blend almond flour, dates, rolled oats, shredded coconut, and cinnamon until crumbly.
3. **Assemble:**
    - Layer the peaches in a serving dish and top with the crisp mixture.
4. **Serve:**
    - Enjoy chilled or at room temperature!

Raw Cabbage Slaw with Sesame Dressing

Ingredients

- 4 cups green cabbage, thinly sliced
- 1 cup carrots, grated
- 1/2 cup bell pepper, sliced
- 1/4 cup green onions, chopped

Dressing

- 3 tablespoons sesame oil
- 2 tablespoons soy sauce or tamari
- 1 tablespoon rice vinegar
- 1 teaspoon maple syrup
- 1 teaspoon sesame seeds

Instructions

1. **Prepare Dressing:**
    - In a bowl, whisk together sesame oil, soy sauce, rice vinegar, maple syrup, and sesame seeds.
2. **Combine Salad Ingredients:**
    - In a large bowl, mix cabbage, carrots, bell pepper, and green onions.
3. **Dress Slaw:**
    - Pour dressing over the slaw and toss well.
4. **Serve:**
    - Enjoy chilled!

Raw Nut Burgers

Ingredients

- 1 cup nuts (walnuts, almonds, or pecans)
- 1 cup sunflower seeds
- 1/2 cup flaxseed meal
- 1 cup grated carrot
- 1 teaspoon cumin
- Salt and pepper, to taste

Instructions

1. **Blend Ingredients:**
    - In a food processor, combine nuts, sunflower seeds, flaxseed meal, grated carrot, cumin, salt, and pepper. Pulse until a dough forms.
2. **Form Patties:**
    - Shape the mixture into burger patties.
3. **Dehydrate (optional):**
    - For a firmer texture, dehydrate in a dehydrator for a few hours.
4. **Serve:**
    - Enjoy on lettuce wraps or with your favorite toppings!

Coconut Water and Berry Smoothie

Ingredients

- 1 cup coconut water
- 1 cup mixed berries (fresh or frozen)
- 1 banana
- 1 tablespoon chia seeds

Instructions

1. **Blend Ingredients:**
   - In a blender, combine coconut water, mixed berries, banana, and chia seeds. Blend until smooth.
2. **Serve:**
   - Pour into glasses and enjoy immediately!

Raw Zucchini Fritters

Ingredients

- 2 cups grated zucchini (squeeze out excess moisture)
- 1/2 cup almond flour
- 1/4 cup nutritional yeast
- 1 teaspoon garlic powder
- Salt and pepper, to taste

Instructions

1. **Mix Ingredients:**
    - In a bowl, combine grated zucchini, almond flour, nutritional yeast, garlic powder, salt, and pepper.
2. **Form Fritters:**
    - Shape the mixture into small patties.
3. **Serve:**
    - Enjoy raw or lightly dehydrated for a firmer texture!

Raw Berry Pie

Ingredients

- 1 cup pitted dates
- 1 cup almonds
- 2 cups mixed berries (fresh or frozen)
- 1 tablespoon lemon juice
- 1 tablespoon chia seeds

Instructions

1. **Make Crust:**
   - In a food processor, blend dates and almonds until a sticky dough forms. Press into the bottom of a pie dish.
2. **Prepare Filling:**
   - In a bowl, mix berries, lemon juice, and chia seeds.
3. **Assemble Pie:**
   - Pour berry mixture into the crust and spread evenly.
4. **Chill:**
   - Refrigerate for at least 1 hour before serving.

Marinated Avocado Salad

Ingredients

- 2 ripe avocados, diced
- 1 cup cherry tomatoes, halved
- 1/4 red onion, thinly sliced
- 1/4 cup fresh cilantro, chopped

Dressing

- 2 tablespoons olive oil
- Juice of 1 lime
- Salt and pepper, to taste

Instructions

1. **Prepare Dressing:**
   - In a bowl, whisk together olive oil, lime juice, salt, and pepper.
2. **Combine Salad Ingredients:**
   - In a large bowl, mix diced avocados, cherry tomatoes, red onion, and cilantro.
3. **Dress Salad:**
   - Pour dressing over the salad and toss gently.
4. **Serve:**
   - Enjoy fresh!

Raw Chocolate Energy Bars

Ingredients

- 1 cup pitted dates
- 1 cup nuts (almonds or walnuts)
- 1/2 cup raw cacao powder
- 1/4 cup shredded coconut
- Pinch of salt

Instructions

1. **Blend Ingredients:**
   - In a food processor, combine dates, nuts, cacao powder, shredded coconut, and salt. Blend until a sticky mixture forms.
2. **Press into Pan:**
   - Press the mixture into a lined baking dish to form a flat layer.
3. **Chill:**
   - Refrigerate for at least 1 hour to set.
4. **Cut and Serve:**
   - Cut into bars and enjoy as a healthy snack!

Enjoy these delicious raw recipes!

Raw Pumpkin Seed Hummus

Ingredients

- 1 cup raw pumpkin seeds
- 1/4 cup tahini
- 2 tablespoons lemon juice
- 1 clove garlic
- 1 teaspoon cumin
- Salt, to taste
- Water, as needed

Instructions

1. **Blend Ingredients:**
    - In a food processor, combine pumpkin seeds, tahini, lemon juice, garlic, cumin, and salt. Blend until smooth.
2. **Adjust Consistency:**
    - Add water as needed to achieve your desired consistency.
3. **Serve:**
    - Enjoy with raw veggies or crackers!

Fresh Herb Pesto

Ingredients

- 2 cups fresh basil leaves
- 1/2 cup walnuts or pine nuts
- 1/4 cup nutritional yeast
- 2 cloves garlic
- 1/2 cup olive oil
- Salt and pepper, to taste

Instructions

1. **Blend Ingredients:**
    - In a food processor, combine basil, nuts, nutritional yeast, and garlic. Pulse until finely chopped.
2. **Add Olive Oil:**
    - With the processor running, slowly drizzle in olive oil until smooth.
3. **Season:**
    - Add salt and pepper to taste.
4. **Serve:**
    - Toss with zucchini noodles or use as a spread.

Raw Choco-Nut Brownies

Ingredients

- 1 cup walnuts
- 1 cup pitted dates
- 1/2 cup raw cacao powder
- 1/4 cup almond flour
- Pinch of salt

Instructions

1. **Blend Ingredients:**
   - In a food processor, combine walnuts, dates, cacao powder, almond flour, and salt. Blend until a sticky dough forms.
2. **Press into Pan:**
   - Press the mixture into a lined baking dish to create an even layer.
3. **Chill:**
   - Refrigerate for at least 1 hour to set.
4. **Cut and Serve:**
   - Cut into squares and enjoy!

Spicy Watermelon Salad

Ingredients

- 4 cups watermelon, cubed
- 1/4 cup red onion, thinly sliced
- 1/4 cup fresh mint, chopped
- 1 jalapeño, minced (optional)
- Juice of 1 lime
- Salt, to taste

Instructions

1. **Combine Ingredients:**
    - In a large bowl, mix watermelon, red onion, mint, and jalapeño.
2. **Dress Salad:**
    - Drizzle with lime juice and sprinkle with salt. Toss gently.
3. **Serve:**
    - Enjoy chilled!

Raw Nutty Granola Bars

Ingredients

- 1 cup oats
- 1 cup mixed nuts (almonds, walnuts, etc.)
- 1/2 cup nut butter (almond or peanut)
- 1/4 cup honey or maple syrup
- 1/4 cup dried fruit (raisins, cranberries)

Instructions

1. **Mix Ingredients:**
   - In a bowl, combine oats, nuts, nut butter, honey, and dried fruit. Stir until well combined.
2. **Press into Pan:**
   - Press the mixture into a lined baking dish to form an even layer.
3. **Chill:**
   - Refrigerate for at least 1 hour to set.
4. **Cut and Serve:**
   - Cut into bars and enjoy!

Tropical Fruit Salad

Ingredients

- 1 cup pineapple, diced
- 1 cup mango, diced
- 1 cup kiwi, diced
- 1 cup strawberries, halved
- Juice of 1 lime
- Fresh mint, for garnish

Instructions

1. **Combine Ingredients:**
   - In a large bowl, mix pineapple, mango, kiwi, and strawberries.
2. **Dress Salad:**
   - Drizzle with lime juice and toss gently.
3. **Serve:**
   - Garnish with fresh mint and enjoy!

Raw Chocolate Banana Ice Cream

Ingredients

- 4 ripe bananas, sliced and frozen
- 1/4 cup raw cacao powder
- 1 tablespoon almond milk (or more, as needed)

Instructions

1. **Blend Ingredients:**
    - In a blender or food processor, combine frozen bananas, cacao powder, and almond milk. Blend until smooth and creamy.
2. **Adjust Consistency:**
    - Add more almond milk if needed to reach desired consistency.
3. **Serve:**
    - Enjoy immediately or freeze for a firmer texture!

Raw Sweet Potato Chips

Ingredients

- 2 medium sweet potatoes, thinly sliced
- 2 tablespoons olive oil
- Salt, to taste
- Spices (optional, like paprika or cayenne)

Instructions

1. **Preheat Dehydrator:**
   - If using a dehydrator, set it to 135°F (57°C).
2. **Toss Sweet Potatoes:**
   - In a bowl, toss sweet potato slices with olive oil, salt, and spices.
3. **Dehydrate:**
   - Arrange slices in a single layer on dehydrator trays. Dehydrate for 6-8 hours until crispy.
4. **Serve:**
   - Enjoy as a healthy snack!

Enjoy these vibrant and nutritious recipes!

Raw Almond Milk

Ingredients

- 1 cup raw almonds
- 4 cups water (for blending)
- 1-2 tablespoons maple syrup or honey (optional)
- 1 teaspoon vanilla extract (optional)
- Pinch of salt

Instructions

1. **Soak Almonds:**
    - Soak almonds in water for at least 8 hours or overnight. Drain and rinse.
2. **Blend:**
    - In a blender, combine soaked almonds and 4 cups of fresh water. Blend on high until smooth.
3. **Strain:**
    - Use a nut milk bag or fine mesh strainer to strain the mixture, separating the almond pulp from the liquid.
4. **Sweeten (optional):**
    - Return the almond milk to the blender and add maple syrup, vanilla extract, and salt. Blend briefly to combine.
5. **Store:**
    - Store in an airtight container in the refrigerator for up to 4-5 days. Shake well before using!

Raw Pumpkin Pie Smoothie

Ingredients

- 1 cup pumpkin puree (fresh or canned)
- 1 banana
- 1 cup almond milk (or any plant-based milk)
- 1 tablespoon maple syrup (optional)
- 1 teaspoon pumpkin pie spice
- 1/2 teaspoon vanilla extract

Instructions

1. **Blend Ingredients:**
    - In a blender, combine pumpkin puree, banana, almond milk, maple syrup, pumpkin pie spice, and vanilla extract.
2. **Blend Until Smooth:**
    - Blend until the mixture is smooth and creamy.
3. **Serve:**
    - Pour into a glass and enjoy immediately! Optionally, top with a sprinkle of cinnamon or nutmeg.

Enjoy your delicious raw recipes!

www.ingramcontent.com/pod-product-compliance
Lightning Source LLC
LaVergne TN
LVHW081502060526
838201LV00056BA/2885